Raphael.
Michaelangelo.
Donatello.
Leonardo.

They're short, bow-legged and green. They're pet-store escapees who left the fishbowl slime behind to become the hardest-shelled—and most handsome—superheroes ever to crawl out of a sewer.

Now, see how well you *really* know them!

- Who drew the first Turtle sketch—and what was the character originally called?

- What famous teen star is heard but not seen in the film?

- How many fingers do the Turtles have on each hand?

- What famous comic-book character guest-starred in one of the early Turtles comics?

- How many monsters are there in *Curse of the Killer Pizzas*?

- How many Turtles does it take to screw in a light bulb?

THE UNAUTHORIZED TEENAGE MUTANT NINJA TURTLES QUIZ BOOK

THE UNAUTHORIZED TEENAGE MUTANT NINJA TURTLES QUIZ BOOK

AN UNOFFICIAL TRIVIA
GUIDE TO AMERICA'S
HOTTEST PHENOMENON

JEFF ROVIN

ST. MARTIN'S PAPERBACKS

THE UNAUTHORIZED TEENAGE MUTANT NINJA TURTLES QUIZ BOOK

ISBN: 0-312-92469-0

Printed in the United States of America

St. Martin's Paperbacks edition/June 1990

10 9 8 7 6 5 4 3 2 1

Acknowledgments

The author would like to thank the following for their help in assembling this book:

Brendon Begnal
Eric Berkowitz
Shep Boucher
Zach and Jesse Casey
Aaron and Jay Kaplan
Danny McDougall
Steve Menniti
Ryan and Alec Olszewski
Paul Orlando
Todd Parkin
Logan Perel
Ryan Quirk
Eva Rupert
Nate Sheldon
Trevor Soule
James Steinberg
and Sam, C.B., & Mike

Introduction

Hope you won't mind a short, fun-filled history lesson before we get cooking. Y'see—

Teenage Mutant Ninja Turtles weren't the first super-powered animals. (They may be among the *best*—but that's a different story!)

You've probably heard of a few of these other mighty mammals, insects, and birds. For instance:

■ Hoppy, the Captain Marvel Bunny, who was an ordinary rabbit until he uttered the word "Shazam"! Then he became a costumed, super-powered, crime-fighting hare.

■ Mighty Mouse, the flying, super-strong mouse, who burst onto motion picture screens in 1944 and has been fighting cats and wolves ever since.

■ Ace, the Bat-Hound, Batman's German Shepherd. He slips on a mask to fight crime beside the Caped Crusader, and was introduced in comic books in 1955.

Then there are Underdog, Courageous Cat, Sherlock Monk, the Three Mouseketeers, Super Duck, Atom Ant, Fearless Fly, and many, many more.

And since the creation and phenomenal success of Teenage Mutant Ninja Turtles, there have been more super-animals than ever, such as (yes . . . these are *real* comic book characters):

■ Pre-Teen Dirty Gene Kung-Fu Kangaroos

■ Adolescent Radioactive Black Belt Hamsters

■ Mildly Microwaved Pre-Pubescent Kung-Fu Gophers

- Geriatric Gangrene Jujitsu Gerbils
- Cold Blooded Chameleon Commandos
- Naive Inter-Dimensional Commando Koalas
- Samurai Penguin
- Panda Khan
- Duckbots

. . . and countless others. In fact, in a recent comic book entitled *The Last of the Viking Heroes* (#2), there's a *new* Teenage Mutant Ninja Turtle: his name is Jon, and he's created by a wizard's potion. (See the sections *Fast Facts #'s* 8, 12, 13, and 17 for more on these and other characters.)

Yet, of all these characters old and new, none has caught the public's imagination the way the Turtles have.

Why?

Many reasons.

For one thing, they're likable and we can relate to them—their yearning for junk food, their fun-loving natures, even their bickering.

For another, they're simple, everyday folk, just like us. The only difference is that they happen to be two-legged, talking, martial arts-practicing turtles.

For yet another, they *care* about each other and about every living thing.

Finally, they're brave and heroic—qualities we admire and *hope* we all have somewhere inside of us.

Which brings us to this paperback.

The purpose of the book is twofold. First, of course, we hope to entertain you. And challenge you. (There's some stuff in here which will cause even the greatest Turtles experts to scratch their heads!)

Just as important, however, we want to present an overview of Turtlemania. Our questions and *Fast Facts* commentary were designed to put the Teenage Mutant Ninja Turtles in perspective as a cultural phenomenon.

And what a marvel they are, breaking records in the areas of toy sales, comic book sales, movie ticket sales, videocassette sales, record album sales—you name it, the Turtles have busted it!

Nor are the Turtles a mere fad, this year's Cabbage Patch Dolls or Trivial Pursuit. They're here to stay—original, vital, exciting characters who have the ability to change with the times. (After all, some of their dialogue *will* sound a bit dated in a few years).

Their popularity will become even greater, one must imagine, after the next live-action film is released. (Yes, there's going to be one. It's already in the planning stages.) It's not difficult to imagine a long-lived series of films: after all, look how the James Bond movies have endured!

If you're a Teenage Mutant Ninja Turtles fanatic, this book will test your knowledge of the foursome, their friends, and their creators. (And we do mean *test*. Check out the section *The Creation of the Turtles* and see how many of the questions you can answer!)

If you're merely interested in the Turtles, and want to learn more about them and their world, you've come to the right place!

But *whoever* you are, if you're stumped . . . well, we're not quite as mean as Foot Soldiers: you'll find the answers to all the questions in the back of the book.

We've also got a few surprises for you inside:

special sections with interesting information which will be of interest to anyone who loves the husky green dudes.

A Word About the Multiple Origins of the Turtles—

As you read this book, keep in mind that the Turtles actually had two different origins: one in the original comic book, and a slightly different one in the cartoons.

In the comic book origin, the mutagen fell off a truck as it braked hard, then tumbled down the sewer.

In the cartoon origin, Shredder obtained the mutagen from Krang and poured it down the sewer, inadvertently creating the mutated turtles when he tried to douse Splinter.

Got that? Good. Because—

To further complicate matters, there's the movie origin, which is more like the comic book origin, *and* the Archie Comics comic book origin, which is based on the TV cartoons. And, of course, there are the graphic novels which reprint the original comic books.

So—whenever we talk about specific origins, don't think we're trying to play a shell game!

We're just trying to keep our Turtles straight!

Now, pull up a chair, pick up a slice of pizza, and away we go!

QUESTIONS

Movie Trivia

1. Which character is mugged in the beginning of the film?
   a) April
   b) Raphael
   c) Casey

2. Where does this take place?

3. What Turtle weapon gets left behind after the fight with the muggers?
   a) A sai
   b) A katana
   c) Nunchucks

4. What does Casey use as a weapon to attack the muggers in the park?

5. Early in the movie, Raphael goes out alone. Where does he go?

6. To what street number does Michaelangelo ask that his pizza be delivered:
a) 122⅛
b) 222½
c) 345⁶⁄₇

7. What company delivers the pizzas?

8. Splinter tells April that he and the Turtles have been living in the sewer for how many years?

9. Where have the Turtles gone when Splinter is kidnapped?

10. Which Turtle gets into a rooftop brawl with the Foot Clan?

11. What is the name of April's junk shop?

12. What is the name of the diaper service seen in the beginning of the film? (Hint: Fans of Nintendo® games should have no trouble with this one!)

13. What is the name of the broadcast on which April regularly appears?

14. Ironically, what message is left on April's answering machine during the fire?

15. Where do April, Casey, and the Turtles go after the Foot Clan fight at her apartment?

16. Who is the last one to battle Shredder on the roof?
a) Splinter
b) Michaelangelo
c) Casey

17. Shredder ends up in:
a) Jail
b) Japan
c) A garbage truck

18. How much money is snatched from April's wallet in her apartment?

19. In the first flashback, Splinter says that the first word any of the Turtles uttered was:
a) Da-da
b) Pizza
c) Cowabunga

20. What does Donatello bring to the campfire meditation?

(Answers on p. 107)

The Creation of the Turtles

Teenage Mutant Ninja Turtles were created by Kevin Eastman and Peter Laird, who formed a company to publish the comic book themselves.
What do you know about the creation of the heroes?

1. The cover of the first issue of *Teenage Mutant Ninja Turtles* was inspired by the cover of what comic book?

2. Who was the writer and artist of that inspirational comic book?

3. What did Eastman and Laird call their company?

4. In what city and state did the duo live?

5. What were the two doing when they first came up with the idea for the Turtles?
   a) Watching TV
   b) Eating at a fast food restaurant

c) Browsing through a book about turtles in a bookstore

6. Who drew the first sketch—Eastman or Laird?

7. What year was that?

8. What did he originally call the character?

9. What weapon was the character holding?
a) Nunchucks
b) A sword
c) None

10. What Marvel superhero provided the inspiration for a key scene in the story—a young boy pushing a blind man to safety?

11. The creators named their characters after:
a) Painters
b) Composers
c) Authors

12. How many copies were printed of the first issue of *Teenage Mutant Ninja Turtles*?
a) 500
b) 3,000
c) 10,000

13. How many pages was it?
a) 32
b) 40
c) 58

14. On what day of the month and year did the first issue make its debut?
a) January 20, 1980
b) April 21, 1982
c) May 5, 1984

15. How did Eastman raise the $500 he kicked in to help publish the magazine?

16. True or false: the young men borrowed $700 from Kevin's Uncle Quentin to help pay for the publication.

17. True or false: the first issue was in full color.

18. How long did it take for the first issue to sell out?
a) 3 days
b) 3 weeks
c) 3 months

19. What was the cover price of the comic book?
a) 75 cents
b) $1.00
c) $1.50

20. What is that issue worth today?

21. How many copies of the second issue were printed?
a) 3,000
b) 6,000
c) 9,000

22. What was the first licensed Turtles product to appear in the marketplace?

23. What company manufactured the above?

24. What was the second licensed product?

25. When was Peter Laird born?
a) January 27, 1954
b) January 27, 1958
c) January 27, 1961

26. When was Kevin Eastman born?
a) May 30, 1958
b) May 30, 1960
c) May 30, 1962

27. How much profit did the team make on the first issue of *Teenage Mutant Ninja Turtles*?
a) $400
b) $1,000
c) $5,000

28. How much profit did they make on the second issue?
a) $4,000
b) $7,500
c) $10,000

29. Since #1 of *Teenage Mutant Ninja Turtles* has been reprinted several times, how can you tell if an issue is a bonafide, super-valuable first printing copy?

a) It has a different cover
b) Subsequent printings were in color
c) The inside back cover has an advertisement for *Gobbledygook*.

(Answers on p. 108)

Fast Facts # 1

What do you know about the historical figures whose names were adapted by Eastman and Laird for their Turtles? Read the following to learn a little bit about these fascinating men—

Donatello

His real name was Donato di Niccolo dei Bardi, and he was a Florentine sculptor. He is best known for his bronzes *The Boy David* and his masterpiece, the equestrian statue *Gattamelata*. Donatello lived from 1386 to 1466.

Michelangelo

Spelled Michelangelo, not Michaelangelo, the full name of the great Italian artist was Michelangelo Buonarotti. A sculptor, architect, and painter, he is best known for his sculptures *David*, the *Pieta*, and *Moses*, and for his paintings of scenes from the Biblical Genesis on the ceiling of the Sistine Chapel. Michelangelo lived from 1475 to 1564.

Raphael

The real name of this great Italian artist was Raffaelo Sanzio. He painted many works based on mythological themes, and also created portraits and altar pieces. He was also an exceptional architect. Raphael lived from 1483 to 1520.

Leonardo

Leonard da Vinci was one of the greatest geniuses in human history. Not only was he a brilliant artist, but he was also a magnificent scientist, engineer, and architect. His most famous paintings are *Mona Lisa* and *The Last Supper*. The Italian Leonardo lived from 1452 to 1519.

All of these men lived and worked in a period known as the Italian Renaissance, which dates from the middle of the 1300s to the end of the 1500s. It was a period in which culture and science were reborn after stagnating for many long years during the Dark Ages. Renaissance is the French word for "rebirth."

Turtle Weapons

Match the Turtle, hero, or bad guy with the weapon he prefers.

CHARACTER

1. Donatello
2. Raphael
3. Genghis Frog
4. Michaelangelo
5. Rat King
6. Leonardo
7. Leatherhead
8. Baxter Stockman

WEAPON

a. Swamp Gun
b. Snakebelt
c. Nunchucks
d. Sai
e. Anti-Turtle Swatter
f. Staff
g. Katana
h. Tongue Gun

(Answers on p. 108)

Fast Facts #2

You know when they were born (see *The Creation of the Turtles*), but here are some things you may *not* know about Turtles creators Eastman and Laird—

Peter Laird

Laird was born in North Adams, Massachusetts. After graduating from the University of Massachusetts (Amherst) in 1976 with a Bachelor of Fine Arts Degree, he opened a used-book store in nearby Northampton. He also created freelance drawings for the local newspaper, *The Daily Hampshire Gazette*, and published a short-lived comic book inspired by Conan entitled *Barbaric Fantasy*.

Three years later, he made his first foray into publishing by founding the cartoon magazine *Scat*.

Laird gave up the bookstore business in 1981, left *Scat*, and moved to Dover, New Hampshire, where his wife-to-be Jeannine Atkins was attending college. It was about that time Laird met—

Kevin Eastman

Eastman is a native of Portland, Maine and, after graduating from high school, he spent a short time at the Portland School of Art and the University of Southern Maine. An aspiring artist, he was earning a meager living writing and illustrating stories for *Comix Wave* magazine. In the fall of 1982, he happened to notice a copy of *Scat* which had been left on a bus. Thinking it might be a good outlet for his art, he went up to the *Scat* offices. Though Laird had left the publication, a staff member was struck by how closely Eastman's art resembled that of Laird, and got the two together.

The young men discovered they had a great deal in common—not just art style, but also a passion for the artwork of comic book great Jack Kirby *(Captain America, Thor, The Fantastic Four)*. They became close friends and, after three years, got enough money together to create a comic book: issues #1 and #2 of *Gobbledygook* were published in 1984, the first Mirage Studios magazine.

Can anyone guess what the second was?

Order, Order!

If you're a longtime reader of the Turtles comic books, then you'll know which characters were introduced when.

Arrange the names in the list below so that they match the order in which the characters first appeared in the Turtles graphic novels.

April O'Neil
Tang Shen
Hamato Yoshi
Shredder (in his civilian identity)
Splinter
The Turtles
The Purple Dragon Gang
The Foot Clan
Baxter Stockman

(Answers on p. 109)

Fast Facts #3

If *you* were going to create a team of Japanese-based animal superheroes, which classes would make acceptable good and bad guys, other than *ninja?*

Well, other orders of ancient Japan include *daimyos*, the provincial lords; *shoguns*, the equivalent of modern generals; *samurai*, a hereditary warrior class; *ronin*, *samurai* who had no master; *bushi*, who were warriors in general; the *yakounine*, who were police officers; *betos*, who were a cut above the criminal class; and *yakuza*, who *were* criminals!

I'm a Star!

With the Turtles a hit, Eastman and Laird branched out into other titles, in addition to the regularly published *Teenage Mutant Ninja Turtles*. See what you know about some of these.

1. After the third issue of *Teenage Mutant Ninja Turtles* was published, each of the Turtles was given his own magazine. Which grouping below represents the correct order in which these were published?
   a) Michaelangelo, Raphael, Donatello, Leonardo
   b) Raphael, Michaelangelo, Donatello, Leonardo
   c) Donatello, Leonardo, Raphael, Michaelangelo
   d) Leonardo, Michaelangelo, Raphael, Donatello

2. A second title featuring all of the Turtles was introduced in May of 1987. Its name was:

a) *Tales of the Teenage Mutant Ninja Turtles*
b) *The Legend of the Teenage Mutant Ninja Turtles*
c) *The Teenage Mutant Ninja Turtles and Shredder*
d) *The World of the Teenage Mutant Ninja Turtles*

3. What error on 500 copies of *Teenage Mutant Ninja Turtles* #3 has made those copies collector's items?

4. What dinosaur characters did Laird co-create with artist Steve Bissette in 1988?

5. When did the first issue of Archie Comics' all-new *Teenage Mutant Ninja Turtles* first appear?

6. Who drew the issue?

7. Where did Shredder set up headquarters in that issue?
a) Mike's Garage
b) The Gangsterland Museum
c) Slash 4 Cash Gym

(Answers on p. 109)

Fast Facts #4

Where in the world did the expression "cowabunga" originate?

It was first used by the TV character Chief Thunderthud, the Indian founder of Doodyville, who was seen on the TV series *The Howdy Doody Show*, which aired on Saturday mornings from 1947 to 1960.

Unfortunately, no one but Thunderthud (and the Turtles) knows *exactly* what it means.

The Motion Picture: Facts and Figures

Good Morning America's Joel Siegel raved that the movie "charmed the shell out of me!" (That's funny, Joel). The *LA Times* syndicate critic, Ben Kallen, noted that the Turtles are "the most popular heroes this side of the Batcave."

The movie has broken box office records everywhere. You've seen it three or four times . . . but how much do you *really* know about it?

1. Exactly how long does the film run?
   a) 86 minutes
   b) 93 minutes
   c) 107 minutes

2. How much money did the film take in on its opening weekend?
   a) $10.6 million
   b) $17.2 million
   c) $25.4 million

3. How much did the film cost to make?
   a) $6 million
   b) $12 million
   c) $20 million

4. Which company distributed the film?
   a) New Line
   b) MGM
   c) Paramount

5. The Turtles were brought to life on the screen thanks to the technical skills of which of these organizations?
   a) George Lucas's Industrial Light and Magic
   b) Walt Disney Productions
   c) Jim Henson's Creature Shop

6. What is the process of animating the Turtles called?
   a) Technotronics
   b) Turtlemation
   c) Animatronics

7. What is the film rated?
   a) G
   b) PG
   c) PG-13

8. *Teenage Mutant Ninja Turtles* had one of the largest opening weekends in movie history. Which number does it rank?

(Answers on p. 109)

Fast Facts #5

Okay, so you know a lot about Teenage Mutant Ninja Turtles. But what do you know about *real* turtles?

Take a look at the info below! It's not as *dull* as you might think! For instance, did you know that—

- There are approximately 250 kinds of turtles?
- The smallest turtle is the bog turtle, which measures three inches long? (Bog Turtle: sounds like the perfect pet for Swamp Thing . . . or a side-kick for Leatherhead!)
- The longest kind of turtle is the leatherback, which is nearly nine feet long and weighs 1,500 pounds . . . that's three-quarters of a *ton*! Pretty impressive, considering the Teenage Mutant Ninja Turtles tilt the scales at around 150.
- The first turtle appeared on the earth 250 million years ago. The animals have changed very little since then.
- Turtle shells are actually made up of two

parts: the upper part, known as the *carapace* (which comes from the Spanish word for "shield"), and the lower part or *plastron* (from the Italian word for "breastplate").

- Shells are comprised of small, flat, bony plates and are attached to the turtle's spine, rib, shoulders, and hips. *That's* why they don't snap off when you pick turtles up!
- The shells are covered with thin scales known as *laminae*. These are made of material sort of like human fingernails. (Hey! You're on your way to becoming a radical turtle. At least, your fingers and toes are!)
- A deep breath for most turtles can last them *hours*! In fact, some freshwater turtles can stay underwater for days on end without coming up for air. (Assuming they don't burn up oxygen by doing anything very active on the bottom of the water . . . like practicing karate!)
- Gopher tortoises have shovel-like toes which enable them to dig holes up to *twelve feet deep* in the sand! They spend much of the winter in these burrows.
- Turtles have excellent eyesight, hearing, and other senses, and also have what scientists call a "sixth sense": they can find water even when they can't *see* it! Scientists believe that turtles can do this because they can tell the difference between light that's over water and light over land. (That's why the Teenage Mutant Ninja Turtles had trouble finding TechnoDrome in the first cartoon episode. They were underground, where their senses didn't work as well!)

- Unlike our pizza-loving heroes, turtles will eat almost anything, including insects, fish, mice, and even birds.
- And just how *do* turtles eat, since (also unlike the Teen Mutants) they have no teeth? A turtle's beak has sharp edges. To help things along, it tears food apart with its claws.

The Motion Picture: Match the Cast

You know the characters . . . but do you know the people who played them?

See how well you do on the match-quiz below. And if you don't get April, you get twenty lashes with a cold slice of pizza!

CHARACTERS

1. April O'Neil
2. Casey Jones
3. Danny Pennington
4. Charles Pennington
5. Chief Sterns
6. Shredder
7. Tatsu
8. Raphael
9. Michaelangelo
10. Donatello
11. Leonardo

a. Raymond Gerra
b. Toshishiro Obata
c. Judith Hoag
d. Michelan Sisti
e. James Saito
f. Michael Turney
g. David Forman
h. Elias Koteas
i. Joch Pais
j. Jay Patterson
k. Leif Tilden

Extra bonus! What famous teen star was heard but not seen in the film?
a) Kirk Cameron
b) Jason Bateman
c) Corey Feldman

(Answers on p. 110)

The Motion Picture: Match the Crew

The list below contains more names than there are titles.

The reason? Because several people contributed their talents to certain aspects of the film. For example, two men wrote the screenplay.

This one's tough. . . .

1. Director
2. Screenwriters
3. Stunt coordinator and martial arts choreographer
4. Music (non-rock score)
5. Producers

a. David Chan
b. Steve Barron
c. Kim Dawson
d. Todd W. Langen
e. Simon Fields
f. Bobby Herbeck
g. John Du Prez
h. Pat Johnson

And come Oscar time, you can probably expect these talented folks to be overlooked by the fantasy-snubbing Academy of Motion Picture Arts and Sciences:

- Director of photography John Fenner
- Art director Gary Wissner
- Production designer Roy Forge Smith
- Set designer Jerry Hall
- Costume designer John M. Hay

(Answers on p. 110)

Fast Facts #6

Could some kind of mutagenic ooze *really* instantly transform animals into people?

Not with present technology. But it *may* be possible in the future. Here's what scientists can do right now.

There are two general kinds of techniques (also known as biotechnologies) which are used to create genetically altered life forms: DNA recombination and plasmid transfer.

What do these mean?

DNA stands for Deoxyribonucleic acid. It's the stuff that determines hereditary characteristics in living things—that is, everything from the color of your hair to the location of your various body parts.

DNA looks like a giant ladder which has been twisted like a corkscrew. To recombine or "splice" a strand of DNA (which determines specific characteristics—say, what a turtle looks like) to another strand (which determines different characteristics—what a person looks like, for example) is a very difficult, time-consuming, and expensive procedure. We don't have any green glob that can do it all by itself. . . . yet.

Plasmid transfer is a different kind of process in which scientists literally knit together loops of DNA. It isn't as complex as DNA recombination, but it doesn't have quite so many uses, either.

Now, all we Turtlemaniacs have to do is be patient! You can't really blame scientists if they're busy trying to breed helpful kinds of bacteria and insects instead of manufacturing mutant turtles and rats. . . .

Turtles on TV

1. When did *Teenage Mutant Ninja Turtles* first appear on TV (month and year)?

2. What was the name of the feature-length Turtles cartoon which introduced the animated characters?

3. What's the first thing we see in the opening titles for the TV show?
a) A manhole cover
b) A police car
c) Buildings with the moon overhead

4. Who is the first turtle seen in the opening titles?

5. What word is used to describe Shredder in the opening song?
a) Evil
b) Ruthless
c) Mad

6. When the pizza is thrown at the viewer in the opening, which three of these ingredients do *not* stick on the screen?

a) Anchovies
b) Onions
c) Pepperoni
d) Mushrooms
e) Green peppers

7. What word is used to describe the turtles "fighting team" in the theme music?
a) Wild
b) Fearsome
c) Cool

8. While Donatello is operating the super machine in the opening titles, what object is sitting right in front of him, under the machine?
a) A coffee cup
b) A newspaper
c) A pizza

9. On the videocassettes cartoon collections, which one of these cartoon series is *not* advertised?
a) *Pound Puppies*
b) *Mad Scientist*
c) *Alvin and the Chipmunks*

10. The company which produces the videocassettes is called FHE. What do these initials stand for?

11. Since its debut, the Turtles cartoon show has consistently ranked #2 in the ratings behind which cartoon series?

(Answers on p. 110)

Fake TV Turtles

Below, in each group of three, there's one title which doesn't belong. Why? Because it's not the name of a real Turtle cartoon episode!

See if you can ferret out the fakes.

1. a) *New York's Shiniest*
   b) *Cowabunga, Shredhead*
   c) *Turtles, Turtles Everywhere*

2. a) *Case of the Killer Pizzas*
   b) *Pizzas from Outer Space*
   c) *The Shredder is Splintered*

3. a) *The Return of Shredder*
   b) *Enter: the Fly*
   c) *No Anchovies, Please*

4. a) *The Great Boldini*
   b) *April Foolish*
   c) *Baxter's Back!*

5. a) *Sky Turtles*
   b) *Turtle Trek*
   c) *Invasion of the Turtle Snatchers*

6. a) *Heroes in a Half Shell*
   b) *Sewer Later, Alligator*
   c) *Hot Rodding Teenagers*

7. a) *Rat Trap*
   b) *Invasion of the Turtle Snatchers*
   c) *Make Mine Mondo*

8. a) *Sky Turtles*
   b) *Invasion of the Punk Turtles*
   c) *Shell is for Heroes*

9. a) *Bye, Bye Fly*
   b) *E = MC Shredded*
   c) *A Thing About Rats*

(Answers on p. 110)

Fast Facts #7

We use 'em ourselves, the cool words adopted and uttered by Teenage Mutant Ninja Turtles. But what do the words mean in real, old-fashioned English?

We've told you about "cowabunga," but here's the scoop on the major meanings of the other words:

AWESOME: *adj.*, 1. inspiring awe (an overwhelming feeling of reverence).

DUDE: *n.*, 1. a man who is overly concerned with his clothes and appearance. 2. an easterner who vacations on a ranch.

MONDO: *n.*, 1. in Zen, a question which a student must answer immediately. In Japanese, *mon* means "question" and *do* means "answers." The word was popularized by the 1963 Italian film *Mondo Cane*.

RADICAL: *adj.*, 1. fundamental; pertaining to the origin of something. 2. extreme.

RIGHTEOUS: *adj.*, 1. morally good and upright.

Turtle Toys

1. Name the company which produces the Turtle figures.

2. Without measuring (don't cheat!), how tall are the Turtle figures?

3. Part of the Turtle toy lineup is a rabbit known as Usagi Yojimbo. This character appeared in his own comic book, and was not created by Eastman and Laird. Who came up with the heroic hare?

4. What's the name of the Random House board game?

5. Which one of these vehicles—made from inner tubes—is *not* part of the Turtles' arsenal?
   a) Sewer Party Tube
   b) Sewer Army Tube
   c) Sewer Battering Tube

6. What did the Turtles use to create a sidecar for the Turtlecycle?
a) A trashcan
b) A wheelbarrow
c) A washing machine

7. The Flushomatic High-Tech Turtle Torture Trap has toilet tissue which absorbs what?

8. What red symbol appears on the top of the Flushomatic?

9. What is pictured on the proof-of-purchase seal on each Turtle action figure package?

10. Fill in the blank: the ooze weapon is called the _____catapult.

11. What is the name of the Turtle surfboard?
a) Sewer Sled
b) Cheapskate
c) Radical Roller

12. The surfboard comes with a shield; what is it made from?
a) A manhole cover
b) A trashcan lid
c) A stop sign

13. On the packaging of the action lineup, what symbol represents a bad guy?

14. What color is the above?

15. What symbolizes a good guy?

16. What color is it?

17. Which action figure is the smallest of them all (without all the attachments)?

(Answers on p. 111)

A Turtles Grab Bag Part I

A selection of questions from all walks of the Turtles mythos!

1. How much money do the Turtles characters rake in for their creators during an average year?
a) $10 million
b) $75 million
c) $350 million

2. Approximately how many companies hold licenses for Turtles products?
a) 100
b) 1,000
c) 3,000

3. Which fast food chain has been selling videocassettes featuring the Turtles?

4. Name the comic book company which publishes the paperback *reprints* of the original *Teenage Mutant Ninja Turtles* comic books:

a) Marvel Comics
b) First Comics
c) Archie Comics

5. Who was the letterer on all the early issues of the original comic book?

6. In the very *title* of one of the Solson Publications *Martial Arts Authorized Training Manual*, how is Raphael's name misspelled?

7. When each of the Turtles briefly had their own comic book titles, how were these series described on the covers?
a) Mini-series
b) Micro-series
c) Limited-issue series

8. True or false: the *current* Mirage issues of *Teenage Mutant Ninja Turtles* are in color.

9. What slight difference is there in the name of the Archie Comics Turtles title, in order to distinguish itself from the Mirage title?

10. What was the editorial page called in early issues of the comic books?
a) Turtle Soup
b) Show and Shell
c) Turtle Tracks

11. How many fingers do the Turtles have on each hand?

12. How many toes do the Turtles have on the front of each foot?

13. In which comic book (title and issue number) did Eastman and Laird salute their hero, artist Jack Kirby, by telling the tale of Kirby, an artist whose drawings came to life?

14. What kind of animal is Rocksteady?

15. In which ear does Bebop wear an earring?

16. After the Turtles fell down the manhole and began to mutate, they learned to speak. In the original comic book, what was the first word uttered by any of the Turtles?

17. Originally, the Turtles' masks were all the same color. What color was this?
a) Blue
b) Red
c) Yellow

18. Who was the only Turtle featured in panel one, page one, of the first Turtles adventure?

19. What is the Rat King's real name?
a) Lafayette
b) Rodentello
c) Ha'ntaan

20. From what country does the Foot Clan hail?

a) China
b) Hong Kong
c) Japan

21. What is Shredder's real name?
a) Oroku Saki
b) Eiji Ginza
c) Michael Osaka

22. Which came first: the Turtles' ability to speak or to stand upright?

23. Here's a doozy: what is co-creator Peter Laird's middle name?

24. True or false: the Turtles have always had their initials on their belts.

25. In the first cartoon, Shredder sent a pair of robots out into the world. The duo's main weapon was:
a) One long tentacle
b) Buzz saws in their feet
c) Propellers which unfolded from their heads

26. What is the most heavily armed vehicle in Shredder's arsenal?

27. In the movie, what song is Donatello humming outside April's farmhouse?

28. What product do the Turtles apply to their sore muscles in the motion picture?

29. According to Splinter, what is a Turtle's worst enemy?
a) Shredder
b) Laziness
c) Anger

30. In the movie, what is Michaelangelo chewing on while he waits for the pizza delivery person?

31. According to the cartoon episode *Bye, Bye Fly*, Krang's home dimension has the _____ in the entire time/space continuum:
a) Most evil beings
b) Most polluted air
c) Worst restaurants

32. In the Mirage comic books, the villainous Gorko is:
a) The fast food additive king
b) A mutant gorilla
c) A circus strongman who only eats turtles

33. In #28 of the Mirage comic book, April is surprised to discover that the farmhouse is located near:
a) One of Shredder's laboratories
b) A nuclear power plant
c) A volcano

34. Which company manufactures the Turtles arcade videogame?

35. In the Archie comics, what is the name of the mad bat who battles the Turtles?
a) Batty Man
b) Wingnut
c) Flap Jack

36. In the Archie comics, which Turtle has been wearing a black costume (to give him an advantage in the dark)?

37. About those Turtle costumes used in making the movie—each one weighed:
a) 25 pounds
b) 45 pounds
c) 70 pounds

38. Which famous feature-length Walt Disney cartoon had a "pleasure land" for bad kids, similar to Shredder's warehouse?

39. What are the call letters of April's TV station in the film?

(Answers on p. 111)

Fast Facts #8

Remember some of those other Turtles-inspired super-heroic animal groups mentioned in the Introduction? Here's some info you may find interesting about a few of them.

Adolescent Radioactive Black Belt Hamsters

Sent into space by NASA, the four hamsters mutate after they pass through Radioactive Cosmic Jello. They crash-land in Tibet, where they are trained to become martial arts heroes. The Hamsters are Clint, Chuck, Jackie, and Bruce.

Pre-Teen Dirty-Gene Kung-Fu Kangaroos

Exchange students from Australia are caught in a mishap at the Presto Labs. Organic computer chips merge with their bodies, turning them into kangaroo heroes. The PTDGKFK are: leader Meep, a pro with boomerangs; Kayo, a scientific genius; Matsu Mike, a master of all the martial arts; Mr. K, who is super strong; and Snurfette, who has countless weapons stored in her pouch.

Mildly Microwaved Pre-Pubescent Kung-Fu Gophers

Snoozing in their gopher holes, the foursome is caught in the text-blast of a microwave bomb. The quartet encounters an Oriental hermit nearby, and he schools them in the ways of martial arts. The characters did not have names.

Naive Inter-Dimensional Commando Koalas

The animals live in Australia in a dimension of animals. Rock and roll stars, they play their music a bit too loud one day and go crashing through a dimensional barrier. They land on our world, where they're hired by the military to be secret agents. The Koalas are all named Bruce.

Geriatric Gangrene Jujitsu Gerbils

Created in a lab, the gerbils become superheroes. After a career of some renown, they become old and out-of-shape, and go to a rest home to live. However, they are called from retirement and return—fat and unfit, but willing to do their part for justice! The heroes are Duffer, Geezer, Codger, and Zeke.

Cold Blooded Chameleon Commandoes

Genetic mutations born in a laboratory, the chameleons are trained in the art of self-defense and weaponry by their creator, Dr. Poindexter. The mighty heroes are Rivit, Nerves, Sarge, and Radion.

If you're interested in any of these characters, ask for their magazines at your local comic book shop.

Incidentally, the Turtles themselves were parodied in #1 of the comic book *Boris the Bear* (1986). In it, the Bear slays Leo, Mikey, Donny, and Bob—*aka* the Juvenile Deviant Hard-Shelled Assassins.

The Movie Poster

1. From left to right, in which order are the Turtles pictured?

2. What are they peeking out from under?

3. How many hands are visible?

4. What's the big building seen in the center of the poster?

5. The teeth of just two Turtles are visible. Which two?

6. What colors are the words *Teenage Mutant Ninja Turtles*?

7. Who's the only Turtle looking right at you?

8. True or false: the moon is visible in the sky.

9. True or false: Shredder is pictured in the poster.

10. True or false: the street, as pictured, is bone dry.

(Answers on p. 112)

The Movie Soundtrack

Match the artist with the song title from the soundtrack of the motion picture *Teenage Mutant Ninja Turtles*.

1. M.C. Hammer
2. Riff
3. Hi Tek 3
4. St. Paul
5. Johnny Kemp
6. Spunkadelic
7. Partners in Kryme
8. Orchestra on the Half Shell

a. "Every Heart Needs a Home"
b. "Turtle Power"
c. "This Is What We Do"
d. "Let the Walls Come Down"
e. "Turtle Rhapsody"
f. "Family"
g. "Spin That Wheel"
h. "9.95"

Additional questions:

1. What are the names of the other two cuts on the soundtrack?

2. What is the soundtrack's record label?

3. What was the first single released from the album?

4. What is the name of the lead singer of Hi Tek 3?

5. What was the second single release?

6. The third?

7. What's the subtitle of "Spin That Wheel"?

(Answers on p. 112)

Fast Facts #9

What exactly *is* a *ninja*?

The art of *ninjutsu*—*very* roughly translated as "the art of stealth"—is approximately two thousand years old. It was practiced by *ninja*, men and women who were just like modern-day secret agents. They were hired by lords to sneak into the territory of a rival lord, spy, and sometimes set fires or even assassinate enemies.

Ninja flourished as a very popular and specialized breed from 1200 to 1600 A.D. So highly prized were their skills that they remained within families, passed from generation to generation. The families went so far as to live in remote areas of Japan, such as in the mountains. Their homes were filled with underground passages, secret doors, and trap-doors.

Training for *ninja*hood began when girls and boys were five or six years old. They were trained to be superb athletes, learned to hold their breath for incredibly long times, were schooled in the art of staying *absolutely* still and creating camouflage, and learned many different trades so they could pose as different people in any town they visited (they might be a carpenter in one village, a blind person in another, and a fisher in yet another).

In fact, many *ninjas* actually had different spouses and children in various towns! That's one reason people were so suspicious of each other: they never knew who might be a *ninja*! *Ninjas* also went so far as to hide animals in the woods, dressed *exactly like themselves*. If they were pursued, they would free the animal—say, a monkey—and let it run away. Pursuers would be convinced that the *ninja* had changed form, thus giving rise to the belief that *ninjas* had magical powers.

In addition to skills and tricks, *ninjas* used many gadgets. For example, they had hooks which allowed them to climb straight up the wall of a castle. Others learned to use their cloaks as parachutes, and some were actually able to "hang glide" using large kites. Many employed special shoes and jackets which allowed them to "walk" across water.

However, the most colorful of the *ninja's* tools were his or her weapons. *Testsu-bishi* were small, sharp objects which were dropped on the ground when the *ninja* was being pursued. They would impale the feet of the people giving chase, making it impossible for them to continue. The *shurikin* was also highly prized. These sharp stars and crosses were carried in a pouch and thrown at people. As for knives, the *kyoketsu shogs* was a favorite: it's a hooked knife attached to a length of cord. The rope was used to snare a foe (often around the throat!), and then the knife was used to finish the enemy off.

Other weapons included small knives actually concealed in the *ninja*'s mouth, smoke bombs and firecrackers, hairpins (not only worn by women, but by men posing as women), poison (the *ninja* was a chemist too!) which would do everything from kill to put someone to sleep to make them laugh uncontrollably, breathing tubes for hiding underwater, a staff which usually had a hollow end containing a knife, chain (*kusari gamma*, particularly effective in tangling up swords), or chemicals.

The original name for the art of the *ninja* was not *ninjutsu*, but *shinobi*.

Supporting Characters

1. According to the toys, Leatherhead was created by orange mutagen. According to the Archie comics, he was created by:
   a) A witch
   b) Shredder
   c) Orange mutagen

2. What is Leatherhead's real name?

3. Don Turtelli is a local:
   a) Pizza shop owner
   b) Reporter
   c) Mobster

4. Sergeant O'Flaherty mistakenly believes that the Turtles are:
   a) People in costumes
   b) An illusion
   c) Leprechauns

5. What is the name of April's boss in the cartoon series?
a) Mr. Thompson
b) Mr. Shooter
c) Mr. Colon

6. Who is April's boss in the movie?
a) Mr. Levitz
b) Mr. Pennington
c) Mr. DeFalco

7. What is the name of his son?

8. In the cartoon, who is the receptionist at the TV station?

9. The shape of her eyeglasses is:
a) Round
b) Heart-shaped
c) Square

10. How many long tentacles does Krang have?

11. What is the name of the evil gang of Turtle imposters?
a) Teenage Mutant Criminal Turtles
b) Robbers in a Half Shell
c) Crooked Ninja Turtle Gang

12. Baxter Stockman's favorite phrase, "Help me!", is from what famous motion picture?

13. True or false: Genghis Frog worked for Shredder before becoming a hero.

14. Commander Mozar belongs to what alien race?

15. Featured in the comic books is a captain of the NYPD. His name is:
a) Farrillo
b) Harrison
c) Infantino

16. What famous comic book character guest-starred in one of the early Turtles comics (#8)?
a) Cerebus the Aardvark
b) Spider-Ham
c) The Incredible Hulk

17. In the comics, which character keeps a diary?

18. What does Casey Jones wear to cover his face?

19. In which of the cartoons does Shredder first meet Baxter Stockman?

20. What is Splinter's favorite food?
a) Fish eggs
b) Cheese
c) Lettuce

21. The military group commanded by General Traag is known as:
a) The Traag Racers
b) The Rock Soldiers
c) The Danger Corps

22. The Foot Soldier action figures wear armor made from:
a) Turtle shells
b) Sewer bricks
c) Meteorites

23. What is the name of the Turtle villain who feeds on human blood?
a) The Leech
b) The Vampire Bat
c) Bloodsucker

24. What does the abovementioned character do to Raphael?
a) Turns him back into an ordinary turtle
b) Makes him an evil slave
c) Locks him up in a blood bank

25. In the motion picture, with what does Casey Jones attack Raphael when they first meet?
a) A baseball bat
b) A tree limb
c) A golf club

(Answers on p. 113)

The Punk Frogs

The cartoon adventure *Invasion of the Punk Turtles* introduced four mutated frogs, each of them named after an infamous tyrant or madman. Their names are listed below, along with four different weapons; match the frog to his weapon.

1. Napoleon
2. Attila
3. Genghis
4. Rasputin

a. Axe
b. Bow and Arrow
c. Whip
d. Mace

(Answers on p. 113)

The Nintendo® Games Videogame

1. Name the manufacturer of the videogame played on the NES (Nintendo Entertainment System).

2. What's the name of the weapon which fires energy beams powerful enough to knock out almost any foe in the NES game?

3. What kind of barriers block the Turtles in the underwater level of the NES game?

4. In that level, they're trying to find eight things. What are they?

5. Do the Turtles have different colored masks in the NES game?

6. In the NES game, what is the name of the turtle who is disguised to look like the real Turtles?

7. What is the name of the flaming creature in the NES game?

8. Fill in the blank: advertisements for the game challenged players to "Turn Your House Into a _____."

9. What gives the Turtles strength in the NES game?

10. Who must be rescued in Area One of the NES game?

11. Who is kidnapped in Area Three of the NES game?

12. True or false: the Party Wagon does not appear in the NES game.

13. Fill in the blank to complete the character's name: _____ Maniac.

14. True or false: the Turtles cannot lose their own special weapons.

15. What is the name of the weapon which can be used to turn Splinter back into a man?
a) The Re-mutator
b) The Transmogrifier
c) The Life Transformer

16. Which one of these can the Turtles acquire in addition to their special weapons?
a) Boomerangs
b) Invisibility potion
c) Jet-packs

(Answers on p. 113)

The Hand-Held Videogame

1. Which company manufactures the hand-held videogame?

2. What's the name of the key in the handheld game?

3. What is the name of the reef in the hand-held game?

4. What's the name of the little flying creature?

5. The Escape Proof Lock and Chain are named after what famous escape artist?

6. What is the captive April saying on the package?
a) "Go, Turtles"
b) "Help me"
c) "Look out"

7. What color is the game? (That's a gift . . . almost like asking "What was the color of George Washington's white horse?")

8. How many players can play the game?

(Answers on p. 114)

Fast Facts #10

Ever wonder what the difference is between the various major forms of martial arts? Wonder no more!

Karate

Karate literally means "empty hand," and was born on Okinawa in the Ryukyu Islands prior to the 1600s. The hand is the chief weapon: in olden days, it was toughened by pounding it into straw, wet sand, then tree trunks. Flying kicks were later added in order to attack enemies on horseback, and the use of farm tools as weapons was also developed so that Okinawans were equipped to battle armed Japanese invaders.

Kung Fu

This martial arts form began in northern China around 520 AD, in a Shaolin Monastery. It means "person of the highest ability," and was created by a visiting Indian monk named Bodhidharma. There are 1,500 different forms of Kung Fu, but essentially it is boxing with an emphasis on self-defense, your attack depending upon whatever your opponent does. Many practitioners emphasize moving in a circle to avoid blows and get behind an opponent, and using the palm of the hand for attack. Various forms of the art permit weaponry—such as nunchucks.

Jiu Jitsu

When *samurai* found Japan a more peaceful place in the 1800s, and were no longer allowed to carry swords, they had to find another way to defend themselves against outlaws and *ronin*. They adopted a form of combat which was at least two thousand years old. Jui Jitsu means "gentle art," and its essence is on placing opponents in locks by immobilizing or, if necessary, dislocating their joints or breaking. (That *is* gentle, compared to shoving a sword through someone!)

Taekwon-do

Created centuries ago in Korea, *taekwon-do* means "to kick with the feet" (*tae*), "to punch with the hand" (*kwon*), and "method" (*do*). It is approximately 1,300 years old, and was created by a Buddhist monk named Won Kwang. Though it did evolve independent of other martial arts forms, it is not vastly different from them.

Other forms of combat include *sumo*, a form

of wrestling (no part of the body, other than the soles of the feet, may touch the ground); *kyudo*, the use of bow and arrow; *naginata*, combat with a pole or a pole with a blade mounted on the end; *iai-do* and *kendo*, which are battle using swords; and *muay thai*, kick boxing from Thailand.

The Trading Cards

1. How many cards are there in the regular non-movie set?

2. How many stickers are there in that set?

3. How many bonus cards do you get in the "Complete Collector's Edition" non-movie set box?

4. What color are the stickers?

5. The regular non-movie cards have turtle-shell borders around the pictures. What kind of borders are on the bonus cards?

6. What is on the *backs* of the stickers?

7. The regular cards consist of art from:
a) The comic books
b) The cartoon series
c) New art, drawn expressly for the cards

8. True or false: the bonus cards are not identified by numbers but by letters.

9. What is the title of the first card in the non-movie series?
a) "The Epic Begins"
b) "The Saga of the Teenage Mutant Ninja Turtles"
c) "It Began in Japan . . ."

10. What company manufactured the non-movie and movie trading cards?
a) O-Pee-Chee
b) Fleer
c) Topps

11. How many cards are there in the movie set?

12. What is pictured on the first card?

13. The boxed set of movie cards is limited to how many editions?
a) 2,000
b) 5,000
c) 15,000

14. True or false: the same card company produced the movie and non-movie sets.

(Answers on p. 114)

The Movie Tie-Ins

1. Which comic book company published the official color comic book adaptation of the film?

2. Who wrote the comic book script?

3. Who drew the comic book?

4. To whom was the comic book dedicated?
   a) Eastman and Laird's parents
   b) The film's director
   c) The fans of the Turtles

5. In addition to the Turtles, what one other character was featured on the comic book cover?

6. Who wrote the novel based on the film?

7. Who wrote the storybook based on the film?

(Answers on p. 114)

Fast Facts # 11

Here are some things you may find interesting about the weapons used by the Turtles.

- The sai is usually made of iron, and measures between fifteen and twenty inches long. It is principally used in karate.
- Sai are wielded in pairs, one to defend against an incoming weapon, the other to use for offense.
- Nunchucks (also known as *nunchaku*) were originally agricultural tools, made for flailing rice. Each of the two pieces of wood is between twelve and fifteen inches long.
- Not only are the wooden portions of nunchucks used to attack, but the cord is used for choking enemies.
- The katana was the one weapon which every *samurai* used in ancient Japan. The blades were straight prior to 700 A.D., after which they were curved.

Fast Facts #12

Did you know that the Teenage Mutant Ninja Turtles aren't the only superheroic turtles? (Though they're the coolest and the best!)

Not only that: they weren't the first ones, either!

The father of all turtle superheroes was the wonderful McSnurtle the Turtle, the Terrific Whatzit. This historic character was created by Martin Nadle and made his DC comic book debut in 1944.

Merton was the owner of McSnurtle's General Store in Zooville. Honest but lazy, the turtle was visited by the gods of another planet, who gave him the power of super speed so that he could do good on earth. Whenever he needed to become the Terrific Whatzit, McSnurtle simply slipped off his shell (obviously, he never read *Fast Facts* #5), pulled on a blue and red costume, and went to work!

During the 1950s and 1960s, DC Comics also ran the short, comic strip-style adventures of the tortoise superhero Super-Turtle. These colorful escapades appeared in the Superman family comic books (*Superman, Action Comics, Superman's Pal Jimmy Olsen*, etc.).

Super-turtle could fly, wore a red cape, possessed super strength, had super senses, and was almost always involved in comical situations. For example, after spotting an accident, he was happy to move the truck from Kosdanskio Street to Elm Street, because the police officer couldn't spell Kosdanskio. Another time, he needed a rest and burrowed into the center of the earth . . . only to emerge in China, where he became involved in crime-fighting!

Another heroic turtle was Hanna-Barbera's Touché Turtle, of TV fame. Assisted by the brave but stupid dog Dum Dum, Touché wielded a rapier which he used in the name of justice. Though he was rather clumsy, he always managed to triumph. His animated adventures aired beginning in 1962.

Finally, there was Fastback, alias Timmy Joe Terrapin, a member of Captain Carrot and His Amazing Zoo Crew. Born in Okey-Dokey Swamp, the turtle was so slow he couldn't hold down a job. One day, a meteor plunged down the back of his shell, and Timmy Joe found himself able to run super-fast—and we *do* mean super-fast! He can achieve speeds of up to 1,500 miles per second!

The comic book *Captain Carrot and His Amazing Zoo Crew* was first published in 1982, and lasted twenty issues.

And though they weren't turtles, the characters which started the whole mutant craze are the Marvel Comics heroes *The X-Men*, which was created in 1963 by writer Stan Lee and artist Jack Kirby (the man who was the hero of Laird and Eastman). However, it wasn't until the introduction of the character Wolverine in 1973 that the group's popularity really took off!

Fast Facts #13

Sadly, where there's good there's evil.

In addition to all the superheroic turtles, there was also a super-powered, super-villainous turtle: Turtle Man, a nemesis of the DC superhero the Flash.

When he first appeared in 1945, Turtle Man had no turtle accoutrements: he earned his name by being the slowest crook on earth! (Not exactly a great line of work for a slowpoke, one would think.)

Later, he donned a shell which served as bulletproof armor, and which could be fired like a Frisbee thanks to hidden rockets. He also made himself a ray gun which caused people to move at . . . well, at a turtle's pace!

Grab Bag Part II

1. Which company manufactures the turtle-ishious Teenage Mutant Ninja Turtles cereal?
a) Kellogg's
b) General Mills
c) Ralston-Purina

2. The cereal is in the shape of:
a) Throwing nets
b) Turtle shells
c) Pizzas

3. The marshmallows are shaped like:
a) The faces of the Turtles
b) Weapons
c) The letters "D", "M", "R", and "L"

4. What is Donatello carrying on the box?
a) A spoon
b) A bo
c) April

5. Which one of these is *not* a comic book published by Mirage after *Teenage Mutant Ninja Turtles*?
a) *Rockola*
b) *Gizmo*
c) *Bade Biker & Orson*
d) *Prime Slime Tales*
e) *Frogworld*

6. Baxter Stockman is half-man, half:
a) Wasp
b) Fly
c) Grasshopper

7. What is the name of the official Turtles fan club?
a) Turtle Force
b) The Green Team
c) Shell Heads

8. Where will you find the game *Adventures in Turtleopolis*?
a) In videogame arcades
b) Inside videocassette packages
c) On the back of the Turtles cereal box

9. Which product comes packaged in a box shaped like the Turtles' Super Van?

10. True or false: the origin of the Turtles printed on the backs of the early toy packages was based on the original comics.

11. What color is the robe of the Splinter action figure?

a) Black
b) White
c) Purple

12. True or false: Splinter can graw through brick.

13. What color are the belts on the Turtles action figures?
a) Black
b) White
c) Red

14. In the comics, April O'Neil works for which channel?
a) 1
b) 3
c) 6

15. Which of these honorary titles does April hold in the Turtle hierarchy?
a) Associate Turtle
b) Turtle-in-training
c) Turtlette

16. In one of the cartoons, which title does Shredder use to describe himself?
a) President
b) Supreme Lord
c) Emperor

17. How many Turtles does it take to screw in a light bulb?

18. True or false: the Turtles can climb straight up sheer walls.

19. What is the name of the newsletter of the official Teenage Mutant Ninja Turtles fan club?
a) *Chaos Chronicles*
b) *Reptile Report*
c) *Sewer News*

20. True or false: the cookies manufactured by Delicious come in the shape of the Turtles.

21. How much money did the motion picture pull in during its second week of release?
a) $18.8 million
b) $12.5 million
c) $10 million

22. In one of the Mirage-published comic books, Raphael and Casey went to a heavy metal concert. What was unusual about the musicians?
a) They were aliens
b) They were all dressed like Turtles
c) They all fainted on-stage

23. In the Nintendo Games videogame, players automatically start out as which character?

24. In the film, on what island is Shredder's secret warehouse headquarters located?
a) Ellis Island
b) Roosevelt Island
c) Lairdman Island

(Answers on p. 115)

Fast Facts #14

For those of you who are videogame fans (and what right-thinking fantasy buff *isn't*?), here are some tips on how to win at the Nintendo Games *Teenage Mutant Ninja Turtles*.

- If time is running out, switch over to the character who has the least amount of life left. That way, your weakest character will perish.
- When there are enemies on the floor above you, be Donatello: that way, you can use the stick to poke up at them and kill them.
- If you want to pass Boomerangs on to another character, throw several, switch characters, and have the new Turtle catch them!
- Leonardo uses the least energy.
- Donatello is the best to fight leapers and flying foes.
- If you want to keep your distance from an adversary, use Michaelangelo. His nunchucks have the greatest reach of any weapon when used vertically.

- Jump with care in the sewers of area 3. If you leap too high and hit the blocks, you'll cause damage to your Turtle.
- Areas 4 and 5 offer particularly tough foes at the end. To fight the Mouser at the end of 4, have Donatello attack with his bo. Position the Turtle below the robot's jaw and strike upward. At the end of area 5 (TechnoDrome), you have to battle Shredder's imposing tank. Use Scrolls for the battle, and attack the electrical field first. When that's down, immediately turn your attention to the doorway which is disgorging Foot Clan soldiers. Go after the turrets next (ducking to avoid their fire, of course), then shoot out the Tank's "eye" to destroy it.

Fast Facts #15

My, how the role-playing Turtle game-lineup has grown!

The initial game has spawned others, all of them exciting and well worth a look. They are:

- *Transdimensional Teenage Mutant Ninja Turtles*, set in a "multi-verse" with a world of mutant animals.

- *Teenage Mutant Ninja Turtles Guide to the Universe*, in which their comic book foes, the Triceratons, and many other aliens co-star.

- *Teenage Mutant Ninja Turtles Sourcebook: After the Bomb*, set on a future earth where mutant animals thrive due to a nuclear disaster.

- *Teenage Mutant Ninja Turtles: Road Hogs*, a companion to the post-holocaust game, set on the roads of the western U.S. where new mutant animals and bizarre vehicles are the rule.

- *Teenage Mutant Ninja Turtles: Mutants Down Under*, set in after-the-bomb Australia.

Video Turtles

This one's really for diehard Turtle fans!

Below are all the Turtles videocassettes released to date. Can you put them in their correct order, from the first one released to the most recent?

(Note: if you haven't done *Fake TV Turtles* yet, skip this quiz: you'll learn some of the answers below!)

Cowabunga, Shredhead
Case of the Killer Pizzas
Heroes in a Half Shell
Hot Rodding Teenagers
The Shredder is Splintered

(Answers on p. 115)

Fast Facts #16

Who is the most famous fictional turtle of all time?

It may be the Teenage Mutant Ninja Turtles, but the runner-up has to be the famous Mock Turtle from Lewis Carroll's *Alice in Wonderland*, written in 1865.

In a short segment, Alice meets the sad little Mock Turtle who tells about his childhood with the Master Tortoise, who teaches Alice about math (ambition, distraction, uglification, and derision), and then, with a Gryphon, tries to teach Alice a dance known as the Lobster Quadrille.

However, he never *does* get around to explaining how he came to have the head and hind feet of . . . a pig!

Hi-Tech Turtles

1. What is the name of the robot cop who appeared in one of the Turtles cartoons?
a) REX-1
b) TOBOR
c) CAT

2. What is the name of the robot who works with the Turtles in early issues of their comic book?
a) Robotoid
b) Automan
c) Sal

3. Who created the robot mentioned above?

4. What is the name of the flying machine the Clan uses to grab Turtles from below with mechanical hands?

5. Name the robots created by Baxter Stockman in the comics to catch rats.

6. What is the name of the robotic Turtle action figure?
a) Metalhead
b) Iron Shell
c) Steelback

7. What fuel is used to power the Turtle skateboard?

8. Which of these devices is *not* featured in *Donatello #1*?
a) Gravitic Equalizer
b) Mobile Creep Trapper
c) Portal Permanentizer

9. True or false: the TechnoDrome has never left the planet Earth.

10. In the cartoon *Bye, Bye Fly,* how long ago did the spaceship come to Earth?
a) 50 years go
b) 300 years ago
c) 2,000 years ago

11. In the spaceship, Baxter finds a gun which:
a) Causes time to stand still
b) Turns anything into gold
c) Transforms people into animals

12. In which cartoon episode do the Turtles build their van?

(Answers on p. 116)

Fast Facts #17

Perhaps the ultimate collection of mutant animals was the comic book *Laffin' Gas* #1, published in 1986.

This one had everything! In addition to an appearance by the Pre-Teen Dirty-Gene Kung-Fu Kangaroos (see *Fast Facts #8*), there were:

- *Radioactive Wrestling Rodents*—Bulk Bolshevik, Mr. TV, and The Kung Fu Kid.

- *Colossal Nuclear Bambino Samurai Snails*—Darryl, Eddie, Wilbur, and Koichi.

- *Adolescent Maniacal Samurai Hares*—Freleng, Clampett, Avery, and Jones (named after animators and directors of the Bugs Bunny cartoons).

- *Guerrilla Gophers*—no names, just an army of 'em.

Grab Bag
Part III

1. Which Turtle fancies himself an amateur magician?

2. Where did the hot-rodding teens come from:
   a) Los Angeles
   b) Japan
   c) Outer space

3. Everyone knows that the green mutagen was manufactured by a company named T.C.R.I. But do you know what the initials stand for?

4. Which Turtle is the unofficial leader of the group?

5. Who is the most serious of the Turtles?

6. Who is the smartest of the Turtles?

7. What is the name of a ninja axe?
a) Katana
b) Bo
c) Bisento

8. In what city do the Turtles live?

9. True or false: the Turtles never bathe.

10. *Teenage Mutant Ninja Turtles* #9 featured a story about the characters' youth. What were they called in the story?
a) Kid Turtles
b) Teenage Mutant Ninja Turtles Jr.
c) Pre-Teenage Mutant Ninja Turtles

11. Who does Shredder dispatch to capture the Neutrinos in the cartoon *Hot Rodding Teenagers?*

(Answers on p. 116)

Fast Facts #18

There have been plenty of unusual Turtles products, but here are a few of the *most* unusual:

- In 1986, black T-shirts were manufactured with green, glow-in-the-dark designs.
- Aspiring artists, take note: four years ago, Solson Publications produced a magazine entitled *How to Draw Eastman and Laird's Teenage Mutant Ninja Turtles*. It was a dandy guide indeed!
- Turtle practical jokes: you can get a squirting sewer ring (yum!), disappearing green ink, mutant eggs, and a razzer.
- Sneaker Snaps—to prevent your shoelaces from becoming untied!

What's next, one wonders?

Turtle-Green Liquid Paper?

Green Turtle light bulbs (turn *your* bedroom into a sewer)?

One thing's for certain: Godzilla and Kermit the Frog are no longer the hottest green licenses in the world. . . .

More TV Trivia

Don't do this one if you haven't looked at *Fake TV Turtles* yet: some of the answers are here!

1. What unusual weapons do the Turtles use to help subdue the crook who robs a gem from the City Museum in *The Great Boldini?*
   a) Clay
   b) Snowballs
   c) A fire hose

2. What does Michaelangelo use as a weapon to fight Bebop and Rocksteady in the pizza parlor in *Cowabunga, Shredhead?*
   a) An onion, to make them cry
   b) A pizza cutter
   c) A soda bottle, which he shakes violently

3. What does Bebop do with the graphics disk which causes it to malfunction in *Cowabunga, Shreadhead?*
   a) He spills milk on it
   b) He exposes it to mutagen

   c) He puts it into the holographic synthe-
      sizer backwards

4. In that same episode, Shredder threatens
to use the Turtles shells as:
a) Hubcaps
b) Soup bowls
c) Floor tiles

5. True or false: Michaelangelo does a break-
dance in the opening titles of the cartoon
series.

6. How does Shredder contact the Turtles in
Shredder Is Splintered?
a) By phone
b) By TV
c) By sending a hologram image of himself

7. In that same episode, what do the Turtles
use to bury Rocksteady and Bebop?
a) Mud
b) Molasses
c) Cement

8. Here's a real tough one: what is the name
of the movie that's going to be shown on
TV at the end of *Shredder Is Splintered?*

9. What does Irma describe as an emergency
in *The Return of Shredder?*
a) She chips a fingernail
b) Her Walkman breaks
c) She misplaces her glasses

10. At the end of that episode, Shredder carries off which of these characters?
a) Krang
b) Baxter Stockman
c) Rocksteady

11. What is the name of the station boss's girlfriend in *The Return of Shredder*?
a) Paula
b) Boopsie
c) Tiffany

12. Who does Shredder meet in the park in that episode?
a) Muggers
b) A jogger
c) A woman walking her dog

13. What do the monsters' eggs look like before hatching in *Curse of the Killer Pizzas*?

14. In which cartoon does one of the Turtles meet Krang for the first time?

15. What do the Neutrinos hate more than anything?
a) The Turtles
b) School
c) War

(Answers on p. 116)

Weight a Minute!

Can you put the following Turtle characters in their proper order according to weight? Start with the lightest and go to the heaviest.

Metalhead
Usagi Yojimbo
Bebop
Leonardo
Rocksteady
Casey Jones
Raphael
Leatherhead
Genghis Frog
Donatello

(Answers on p. 117)

Fast Facts #19

Teenage Mutant Ninja Turtles is the first live-action movie based on comic book animals which was a box office success!

The previous effort, *Howard the Duck* (1986), based on the Marvel Comics character, was a *huuuuge* flop—though it wasn't as bad as its detractors said. Ironically, *Howard the Duck* cost about a zillion times more to make than the Turtles film!

Incidentally, if you liked the work that Jim Henson and his staff did on bringing the Turtles to life, check out their other non-Muppet fantasy films, *The Dark Crystal* (1983), *Labyrinth* (1986), and their brilliant but little-known effort *Dreamchild* (1985), in which they created live versions of many of the characters from *Alice in Wonderland*.

Grab Bag
Part IV

1. What do the Turtles call their walkie-talk-ies?
   a) Shell Phones
   b) Turtle Communicators
   c) Radical Radios

2. When Krang gets a new body, what causes it to grow to enormous size?
   a) A molecular amplification circuit
   b) A size alternator chip
   c) A mutation control board

3. This body is also remarkable because it can grow:
   a) Wings
   b) Two extra arms
   c) A metal skin

4. What word is written on the side of the Turtle Blimp?
   a) Cowabunga
   b) Turtles
   c) There is nothing written on the side of the Blimp

5. How many blades are attached to the back of each of Shredder's hands?

6. What game does Splinter enjoy playing with Leonardo?
a) Chinese Checkers
b) Monopoly
c) Chess

7. The fly that is merged with Baxter Stockman comes from:
a) A horse stall in a barn
b) A garbage barge
c) A trash can in an alley

8. True or false: Michaelangelo can carry a pizza on his head.

9. Splinter earned his name because of his ability to:
a) Split wooden boards with his fists and teeth
b) He removed a splinter from one of the Turtles when he first met them
c) He was wearing a splint when he first discovered the Turtles

10. True or false: Splinter was once Shredder's student.

11. What do the Turtles put on their pizzas in the morning?
a) Oatmeal
b) Orange slices
c) Dry cereal

12. Shredder merged a pair of animals with his henchmen to create the Bebop and Rocksteady we know and hate. From where did he get the animals?
a) An African jungle
b) The Central Park Zoo
c) He created them in the TechnoDrome lab

13. Beneath their armor and uniforms, the Foot Soldiers are actually:
a) Mutated animals
b) Normal humans
c) Robots

14. What item will you never find Splinter without?
a) His walking stick
b) A gold ring given to him by his own master
c) A pouch filled with soil from Japan

15. True or false: the Turtles always sleep in their masks.

16. What color are Bebop's sneakers in the cartoon series?
a) Black
b) Blue
c) Red

17. What is the name of the news broadcast on which April O'Neil is featured?
a) Live at Five
b) Happy Hour News
c) April in New York

18. Where were the farm scenes of the Turtles movie filmed?
a) Bethel, Connecticut
b) Des Moines, Iowa
c) Wilmington, North Carolina

19. On what date did the movie open?
a) March 23
b) March 29
c) April 6

20. In how many theaters did the motion picture play on opening day?
a) 1,001
b) 1,509
c) 2,006

21. In the cartoon *Heroes in a Half Shell*, which one of these villains was *not* part of the group which attacked April in the opening scene?
a) Bebop
b) Rocksteady
c) Shredder

(Answers on p. 117)

Fast Facts #20

To set the record straight:

Turtles are reptiles, *not* amphibians. They belong to the same class of animal as snakes and crocodiles—not frogs and salamanders.

As for the difference between tortoises and turtles, a tortoise is a turtle that lives on land or in fresh water.

The Last of the TV Trivia

1. What causes the eggs to hatch in *Curse of the Killer Pizzas*?
   a) Microwave ovens
   b) Rocksteady's laser beams
   c) Sunlight

2. In *Enter: The Fly*, Baxter and a Fly are merged in which of these devices?
   a) A teleportation pod
   b) A disintegrator unit
   c) An atom smasher

3. In that episode, what are the Turtles wearing when they go to the greenhouse?
   a) Trenchcoats
   b) Robes
   c) Overalls

4. How many monsters are there in *Curse of the Killer Pizzas*?

5. What incredible power do the other-dimensional monsters possess?

a) They can burn through anything
b) They can fly
c) Their vision causes living things to stand still

6. What does Baxter Stockman plan to do to the Turtles at the end of *Enter: The Fly*?
a) Vaporize them with a laser beam
b) Drown them in tomato sauce
c) Send them forward in time

7. To what building are the Turtles headed at the beginning of that episode?
a) The United Nations
b) April's apartment
c) The World Trade Center

8. *Invasion of the Punk Frogs* introduced a police group devoted to arresting the Turtles (who are wrongly presumed to be outlaws). Their name was:
a) The Anti-Turtle Attack Squad
b) The Turtle Trapping Team
c) SWAT (Secure Wayward Aggressive Turtles)

9. What symbol did these uniformed officers wear on their chests?

10. Whose hand is on the screen in the opening titles when Shredder's blades rip through the picture?
a) Splinter's
b) Leonardo's
c) Michaelangelo's

11. In *Invasion of the Punk Frogs*, from which of the states do the frogs hail?
a) New York
b) California
c) Florida

12. What is the name of the device Shredder has used to disguise himself on occasion in the cartoons?
a) A holographic projector
b) An illusionator
c) A disguise-a-tron

13. In *April Foolish*, April attends a costume party dressed as:
a) A Teenage Mutant Ninja Turtle
b) A rock singer
c) A princess

14. What kind of device does Shredder turn on our heroes in *Sky Turtles*?
a) An anti-gravity device
b) A wind-making machine
c) Mutagen, which gives them pigeon wings

15. How many arms do the aliens have in *Invasion of the Turtle Snatchers*?
a) 4
b) 6
c) 8

16. In which cartoon does April meet the Turtles for the first time?

a) *Heroes in a Half Shell*
b) *Rat Trap*
c) *April Foolish*

17. In *Heroes in a Half Shell*, what does the old lady pull from her shopping cart?
a) Nunchucks
b) A knife
c) A gun

18. What famous movie star does Raphael impersonate in that cartoon?
a) Humphrey Bogart
b) Charlie Chaplin
c) Cary Grant

19. What superhero does Raphael wish were with them when they're searching for TechnoDrome?
a) Superman
b) Tarzan
c) Conan the Barbarian

(Answers on p. 118)

Fast Facts #21

Did you know that there was once a real-life Casey Jones?

He's the hero of a ballad written in 1909 by T. Lawrence Seibert and Eddie Newton. It was inspired by the real-life saga of John Luther Jones of Cayce, Kentucky (hence, the nickname "Casey"), the 36-year-old engineer of the Cannonball Express of the Illinois Central Railroad.

On April 29, 1900, fearing an impending wreck, Casey ordered everyone to leave the train—though he, himself, remained at the controls and died in the crash.

Truly, the new Casey is a hero worthy of such a brave name!

And Finally—

If you're a creative type who likes to do what Eastman and Laird did—that is, sit around thinking up ideas—don't let anyone discourage you, regardless of your age or education! All you need to come up with nifty new characters of your own is imagination. Consider the following:

- Two teenagers—Jerry Siegel and Joe Shuster—created Superman back in the 1930s. Not only that, but it took them *years* to convince someone to publish the character!
- Another teenager, Bob Kane, created Batman.
- Walt Disney had been fired from a cartoon series he was producing. In an effort to save his fledgling studio, he came up with a new character: Mickey Mouse.
- Sylvester Stallone spent his last few dollars to see a boxing match, which was where he got the idea for *Rocky*.
- Edgar Rice Burroughs had been a failure at every job he undertook before turning his hand to writing. The first character he created did

okay; the second character he created was Tarzan.

■ Writer/editor Stan Lee's *Amazing Fantasy* comic book was about to be cancelled, so, as a lark, he came up with a nutty superhero called The Amazing Spider-Man. Sales went through the stratosphere.

In short—

The world needs more flights of imagination, and *you* may be the one who comes up with the next great fantasy character.

As Splinter himself might say: "Never give up!"

ANSWERS

MOVIE TRIVIA

1. a
2. In a parking lot
3. a
4. A hockey stick
5. To the movies. He sees the film *Critters*, and doesn't seem overly impressed by it!
6. a
7. Domino's Pizza
8. 15 years
9. To take April home.
10. Raphael
11. 2nd Time Around: Antiques and More
12. Mario's
13. *Eyewitness News*
14. That she's *fired!*
15. To April's farm
16. a
17. c
18. $20
19. b
20. Marshmallows

THE CREATION OF THE TURTLES

1. *Ronin* (this comic book was published by DC Comics)
2. Frank Miller
3. Mirage Studios
4. Dover, New Hampshire
5. a
6. Eastman
7. 1983
8. A Ninja Turtle. Laird added the words "Teenage Mutant."
9. a
10. Daredevil. The Marvel hero became super after doing the same thing!
11. a
12. b
13. b
14. c
15. It was an income tax refund.
16. True
17. False. It was entirely black and white. Only the covers were in color.
18. b
19. c
20. $300 (wow!)
21. b
22. Miniature figurines (they came out at the same time as the second issue of the comic book)
23. Dark Horse Miniatures
24. A role-playing game from Palladium Books
25. a
26. c
27. a
28. a

TURTLE WEAPONS

1. f
2. d
3. h
4. c
5. b
6. g
7. a
8. e

ORDER, ORDER!

1. The Turtles
2. The Purple Dragon Gang
3. Splinter
4. Hamato Yoshi
5. The Foot Clan
6. Shredder
7. Tang Shen
8. Baxter Stockman
9. April O'Neil

I'M A STAR!

1. b
2. a
3. The blue ink is splotchy in places because of improper screening at the printing plant.
4. Commandosaurs, which is set on a distant world where the weapon-laden Commandosaurs battle the evil Terrorsaurs.
5. March, 1989
6. Dave Garcia
7. c

THE MOTION PICTURE: FACTS AND FIGURES

1. b
2. c. What's super-impressive about this figure, incidentally, is that over half the people who went to the theater were children, admitted at relatively low children's prices. If they'd been adults, the film might have bested *Batman* as having had the best opening weekend in motion picture history!
3. b
4. a
5. c
6. c
7. b
8. Tenth. However, it was: the largest spring opening in film history, and had the second highest number of admissions over a weekend (meaning, again, that a ton of people went to see it, even though, again, a lot of them got in at kiddie prices. Only *Batman* ranked

higher. Think Hollywood should be making more movies based on comic book heroes?)

THE MOTION PICTURE: MATCH THE CAST

1. c
2. h
3. f
4. j
5. a
6. e
7. b

8. i
9. d
10. k
11. g

Bonus: c

THE MOTION PICTURE: MATCH THE CREW

1. b
2. d, f
3. h

4. g
5. a, c, e

TURTLES ON TV

1. December, 1987
2. *The Epic Begins*
3. c
4. Michaelangelo
5. a
6. a, b, e
7. b

8. a
9. c
10. Family Home Entertainment
11. *Chip 'n' Dale's Rescue Rangers*. Boo!

FAKE TV TURTLES

1. c
2. b
3. c
4. c
5. b

6. b
7. c
8. c
9. b

TURTLE TOYS

1. Playmates
2. 4½"
3. Stan Sakai
4. *Pizza Power Game*
5. c
6. a
7. Ooze
8. A skull and crossbones
9. A slice of pizza
10. Retro
11. b
12. a
13. A foot
14. Red
15. A turtle shell
16. Green
17. Krang

A TURTLES GRAB BAG PART I

1. c
2. a
3. Burger King
4. b (Archie only publishes *original* comics based on the characters)
5. Steve Lavigne
6. Rafael. Incidentally, the full title is *Martial Arts Authorized Training Manual Rafael Teenage Mutant Ninja Turtle* (phew!)
7. b
8. False. They're still published in black and white!
9. The Archie title is called *Teenage Mutant Ninja Turtles Adventures*.
10. c
11. 3
12. 2
13. *Donatello #1*
14. A rhinoceros
15. His left
16. "Splinter"
17. b
18. Leonardo
19. c
20. c
21. a
22. Speech
23. Alan

24. False
25. a. Not only could the robots grab objects with the tentacles, they formed them into very effective riatas!
26. The TechnoRover
27. *Old MacDonald Had a Farm*—which was written in 1917, in case you music buffs just *had* to know!
28. Turtle Wax
29. c
30. A popsicle stick
31. c
32. a
33. b
34. Konami
35. b
36. Raphael
37. c
38. *Pinocchio* (1940)
39. WTRL

THE MOVIE POSTER

1. Michaelangelo, Leonardo, Donatello, and Raphael
2. A manhole cover
3. Just one
4. The Empire State Building
5. Leonardo and Raphael
6. Green and yellow
7. Donatello
8. False
9. False
10. False. In fact, Donatello's reflection is clearly visible in the water around the manhole.

THE MOVIE SOUNDTRACK

1. c
2. f
3. g
4. a
5. d
6. h
7. b
8. e

1. The other cuts are *Shredder's Suite, Splinter's Tale I & Splinter's Tale II*.
2. SBK Records
3. *Spin That Wheel.* For the record, it made an exceptional debut on the Top 100 Singles chart in *Billboard*, first appearing at #92!
4. Ya Kid K, who is also the lead singer of Techtronic.
5. *Turtle Power*
6. *This Is What We Do.*
7. Turtles Get Real!

SUPPORTING CHARACTERS

1. a. Her name is Mary Bones.
2. Jess Harley
3. c
4. c
5. a
6. b
7. Danny
8. Irma
9. c
10. Two
11. c
12. *The Fly* (1958 version)
13. True
14. The Triceratons
15. a
16. a
17. April
18. A hockey mask
19. *A Thing About Rats*
20. a
21. b
22. a
23. c
24. a
25. a

THE PUNK FROGS

1. c
2. d
3. a (Note: this is different from the weapon the Genghis action figure carries)
4. b

THE NINTENDO GAMES VIDEOGAME

1. Ultra Games
2. The Scroll Weapon
3. Electromagnetic
4. Eight bombs
5. Yes
6. Meka Turtle

7. Fire Freak
8. Sewer
9. Pizza
10. April
11. Splinter
12. False
13. Chainsaw
14. True
15. c
16. a

THE HAND-HELD VIDEOGAME

1. Konami
2. Freedom Key
3. The Great Electro-Barrier Reef
4. Flap Jaws
5. Houdini
6. b
7. Would you believe . . . green?
8. Just one

THE TRADING CARDS

1. 88
2. 11
3. 22
4. Yellow
5. A thin jagged white border, followed by a thin jagged red border, with a fat black border around that
6. Pieces of a puzzle
7. b
8. True
9. a
10. c
11. 132
12. The movie poster
13. c
14. True

THE MOVIE TIE-INS

1. Archie Comics. Mirage published a black-and white edition, which featured additional material.
2. Peter Laird

3. Jim Lawson did the pencils, while Eastman, Laird, and Eric Talbot handled the inks.
4. b
5. Shredder
6. B. B. Hiller
7. Katharine Ross

GRAB BAG PART II

1. c
2. a
3. b
4. a
5. e
6. b
7. a
8. c
9. Teenage Mutant Ninja Turtles Cookies
10. False. It was based on the cartoons.
11. c
12. True
13. a
14. c. However, in the film she works for Channel 3!
15. a
16. c
17. Four if they stand on each others' shoulders; one if Michaelangelo uses his nunchucks.
18. True
19. a
20. True
21. a
22. a
23. Leonardo
24. c. Wonder where they got the name from!

VIDEO TURTLES

The correct order is:

Heroes in a Half Shell
Hot Rodding Teenagers

The Shredder is Splintered
Case of the Killer Pizzas
Cowabunga, Shredhead

HI-TECH TURTLES

1. a. The name stood for Robot Enforcement Experiment.
2. c. He was later known as Fugitoid.
3. Professor Honeycutt
4. Knucklehead
5. Mousers
6. a
7. Pizza, of course.
8. c
9. False. It's been to Dimension X.
10. b
11. c. In fact, he wastes no time turning Shredder into a fly, and Michaelangelo into . . . a gerbil!
12. *Hot Rodding Teenagers*

GRAB BAG PART III

1. Michaelangelo
2. c
3. Techno-Cosmic Research Institute
4. Leonardo
5. Raphael
6. Donatello
7. c. A bo is a staff, and a katana is a sword.
8. New York
9. False. They take showers regularly . . . though, obviously, they don't need shampoo!
10. c
11. The Stone Warriors from Dimension X.

MORE TV TRIVIA

1. b
2. c

3. c
4. a
5. True
6. b
7. c
8. *The Evil Brain From Dimension X*
9. a
10. b
11. c
12. a
13. Meatballs
14. *A Thing About Rats*
15. c

WEIGHT A MINUTE!

Usagi Yojimbo (125 pounds)   Casey Jones (235 pounds)
Donatello (145 pounds)   Rocksteady (240 pounds)
Raphael (147 pounds)   Bebop (265 pounds)
Leonardo (155 pounds)   Metalhead (500 pounds)
Genghis Frog (175 pounds)   Leatherhead (871 pounds)

GRAB BAG PART IV

1. b
2. a
3. a
4. b
5. 2
6. c
7. b
8. True
9. a
10. False. It's the other way around.
11. c
12. b
13. c
14. a
15. False
16. c

17. c
18. c
19. b. And before you say, "Hey! That's a Thursday, and the picture opened on a Friday," don't forget that many cities had evening shows of the movie on Thursday!
20. c
21. c

THE LAST OF THE TV TRIVIA

1. a
2. b
3. c
4. 3
5. a
6. c
7. c
8. a
9. A "no turtles" emblem: a turtle in a black circle with a black line through it.
10. b
11. c
12. a
13. c
14. a
15. b
16. a
17. c
18. a
19. b